Do I keep a gift forever?

Sometimes but not always. The gifts we are given differ with the situations and needs as God wills.

Are there counterfeit gifts?

Yes. See Matthew 24:24 and 1 Timothy 4:1. John tells us to test the spirits (1 John 4:1). In the same way prophecies are to be weighed and tested (1 Cor 14:29).

Are gifts a sign of spiritual maturity?

No. The greater the gift, the more need there is of spiritual maturity but spiritual gifts are not rewards, they are tools for the work. Gifts are given in order to serve Christ.

Can the gifts be abused?

Yes. Gifts must never be used for personal glory. We must always accept and affirm those within the church whose gifts are different from ours. Pushing people into structural vacancies before discovering their gifts is an abuse. Using gifts privately and not for the benefit of the whole body. Above all, lack of love (1 Cor 13).

Does it matter if I discover/use my gift(s)?

Paul says it does (1 Cor 12:1). We are not possessors but stewards of our gifts (1 Pet 4:11) and one day we will be called to give account of our use of them (Matt 25:14-30).

A L
GII
TE!

Frc

C000181127

1 I

2

3 Teaching
4 Exhortation (encouraging, stimulating faith)
5 Generosity (quickness to give or share)
6 Leadership
7 Mercy (compassion, sympathy, kindness)

From 1 Corinthians 12
(in addition to the above)

8   Wisdom (particular insight or understanding)
9   Knowledge (learned or given by God)
10 Faith (to do great or unusual things)
11 Healing
12 Miracles
13 Discerning of spirits (insight to know when God is speaking or at work and when he is not)
14 Tongues (utterance in a language unlearnt)
15 Interpretation of tongues
16 Apostles
17 Helpers
18 Administration (practical organising/doing)

From Ephesians 4
(in addition to the above)

19 Evangelists
20 Pastors (caring for God's people)

From other New Testament passages

21 Celibacy (1 Cor 7:7)

22 Voluntary poverty (1 Cor 13:3)
23 Martyrdom (1 Cor 13:3)
24 Hospitality (1 Peter 4:9-11)
25 Missionary (Eph 3:1-9)

The New Testament lists are in no sense meant to be complete lists. God gives spiritual gifts as he wills in order to equip his church for mission. Many other gifts (eg the gift of intercession in a special way) might be added.

WAYS TO DISCOVER THE GIFTS OF CHURCH MEMBERS

1 Small homegroups which have met regularly for some time might study the material here. Then let each member list the names of the other members and add beside the name the gifts they think each person has been given. The lists can be collected and the gifts people see in each person can be read out. Sometimes quite surprising discoveries are made in this way.

2 Ministers, deacons, elders or those who have opportunity to share on a one-to-one basis with members can discuss the gifts which they see in each person and spend time with people exploring these and helping them to discover and develop their gifts.

3 When new members receive their basic instruction in the Christian faith this should include something about gifts and their use. A sponsor/ 'church friend' for the first year is a great help and can help a person to discover and develop their gifts.

4 The method at the end of this leaflet will be a useful supplement to the above.

A DANGER TO AVOID

It is always tempting for churches to fit a person into a task which needs doing. This is not God's way or will. We must always discover a person's gifts and develop tasks which are suited to their gifting. One of the ways in which we discover the work God wants us to do is to look at the work he has equipped us to do.

STUDY OF 1 CORINTHIANS 12

v1: Does Paul think it important that we know about spiritual gifts?

v3: Is everyone claiming to speak in God's name or by the Spirit necessarily doing so? How can we know?

v4-6: What is Paul's main point here? What other two words does he use for gifts? Why are these verses important for a church?

v7: To whom are gifts given? What do gifts show? Do we possess them or are they lent? What are the gifts for? How do these points speak to our church?

v8-10: Compare with verses 28-30. Do all believers have the same gift? Is there one gift given to every believer?

v11: Who is the giver of all gifts? How does this affect our view on the gifts of others?

v12-13: Paul compares the church to a human body. How does this help you to understand your church? Paul is saying that all believers are one in Christ. How might he say that to your church today?

v14-24: Using your imagination write out more fully the 'cartoons' which Paul draws here, eg the foot sulking in the corner because it is not the hand: the eye pretending to be the whole body etc. What do these 'cartoons' teach us?

v24-26: Paul tells us that God has designed the body so that there should be no division. How can every member have 'equal concern for one another'? Do we really experience verse 26? What should that mean for those who are lonely, unemployed, poor or suffering?

v27: Is this true of our membership? If not, how can we help it to be?

v29-30: What answer does Paul expect to this question? What does it say to us?

Chapter 13: Why does this come between two chapters about gifts?

Write out chapter 13 in your own words in terms of your own situation (eg 'If I am a popular Lay Preacher or Sunday School teacher but don't get on with others in the church ...').

STUDY OF ROMANS 12

v1: In Old Testament times, worshippers offered the dead bodies of animals or birds. What does Paul want us to offer? Why?

v2: 'Don't let the world around you squeeze you into its own mould'. How can we prevent this?

v3: How are we to think of ourselves?

v4-5: What important point is Paul making here? How should gifted members relate to one another?

v6: Why do we all have different gifts?

v6-8: Why do you think this list of gifts differs from that in 1 Corinthians 12? Is it related to the different characteristics or situations of the two churches? Put these verses into your own words. What point is Paul making?

STUDY OF EPHESIANS 4

v1-8: What picture of the local church does Paul draw here?

v11-12: How does Paul relate gifts to people? Who has the ministry or service to perform? Why are leaders given to the church? What is the end result?

v13-1 6: What is the result when all members use their gifts together in the body of Christ?

STUDY OF 1 PETER 4

v10: Who is to use spiritual gifts? What gift(s) are they to use? How, in what spirit?

v11: What two sorts of gifts are mentioned? How are each to be used? Are both being used in your church? What is the final purpose of it all?

ONE WAY OF DISCOVERING SOME GIFTS

Read the following points, and mark yourself out of five for each. If you give yourself five, it will be one of your very strong points. If you give yourself nought or one, it will be one of your very weak points. Enter your marks in the corresponding boxes on the next page.

1 I am good at listening.
2 I enjoy explaining things to others from the bible.
3 I love preaching or talking about Jesus to a congregation/group.
4 I am often used to bring others to Christ.
5 I enjoy administrative work.
6 I feel a deep caring love for those who are ill, and a call to help them.
7 I am handy at most things and adaptable.
8 I am deeply concerned about the world and social affairs.
9 I am usually looked to for a lead.
10 I make helpful relationships with others easily.
11 Others are helped when I teach them things.
12 I love the study and work involved in preparing a message.
13 God has given me a love for others and a longing to win them for him.
14 I can organise well, clearly and efficiently.
15 Others find my presence soothing and healing.
16 I like helping other people.
17 I am active in service in the community.
18 In a group I am often elected chairman or leader.
19 I can encourage others and help bear burdens.
20 I love study and finding out facts.
21 My sermons have clearly blessed others.
22 I find my life is full of opportunities to witness to Christ.
23 I love doing office work and do it thoroughly.
24 I have sometimes laid hands on the sick and they have been helped.
25 I am a practical type of person.
26 I am very aware of the needs of society and feel called to help.
27 When leading something I put a lot of preparation into it.
28 I really care about other people.
29 I have patience in helping others understand Christian things.
30 I feel a clear call to preach.
31 I love to talk to others about Jesus.
32 I am painstaking about details in organisation.
33 I spend time praying for and with sick people.
34 I spend much time helping others in practical ways.
35 I feel God is at work in the world today and I must work alongside him.
36 I am good at delegating work to others in a team setting.

Add up the marks along each line and place the totals in the end column.